# A Cascade
# Of Flowers

# A CASCADE
# OF FLOWERS

*An inspirational guide to choosing and arranging flowers*

JANE NEWDICK

PHOTOGRAPHS BY DI LEWIS

*Blitz Editions*

First published in 1990 by Salamander Books Ltd

Reprinted 1995 for Blitz Editions
An imprint of Bookmart Ltd
Desford Road
Enderby
Leicester LE9 5AD

ISBN 1-85605-280-X

Printed in the Slovak Republic
51774


All correspondence concerning the content of this book should
be addressed to Salamander Books Ltd, 129-137 York Way,
London N7 9LG United Kingdom.


Editor: Krystyna Mayer
Designer: Peter Bridgewater
Photographer: Di Lewis
Illustrator: Vana Haggerty

# CONTENTS

INTRODUCTION
· · · 6 · · ·

BUNCHES AND BOUQUETS
· · · 8 · · ·

FLOWERS FOR SPECIAL OCCASIONS
· · · 24 · · ·

FLOWERS FROM THE PAST
· · · 54 · · ·

TABLES AND MEALTIMES
· · · 70 · · ·

OUTDOOR ARRANGEMENTS
· · · 100 · · ·

FLOWER CARE AND DATA
· · · 116 · · ·

INDEX
· · · 128 · · ·

# INTRODUCTION

*D*ecorating with flowers has never been more popular than it is today. There has been a huge revival of interest in plants and gardens, and flower shops today offer an ever-increasing variety of cut plants. As this book shows, there are no mysterious rules to the new, relaxed way of arranging flowers and the most lavish effects can be achieved with the minimum amount of skill. All that is needed after a few basic techniques have been mastered is a good eye for colour and texture and, of course, a love of flowers.

The following chapters contain dozens of ideas that will help you to enjoy this lovely craft, ranging from bridal bouquets and table decorations, to arrangements for mantelpieces and window seats. The designs are generous but unfussy, colourful without being garish, and all would look just as at home in a city apartment as in a rambling country house. The practical section provides advice on caring for cut flowers, and there are charts listing the characteristics of over 100 flowers commonly used in arranging. So gather up an armful of flowers and foliage, plan a place to put an arrangement, and create your own glorious cascade of flowers.

This rich and elaborate arrangement composed of early summer flowers is inspired by a flower painting from the past. The perfect blooms have been grouped in an appropriately classic urn-shaped vase.

7

# CHAPTER ONE

# BUNCHES AND BOUQUETS

*A* bunch or bouquet of flowers makes the perfect gift. It can be a small posy made from a collection of garden or hedge-row flowers, a sophisticated, formal arrangement of beautiful blooms in a subtle colour scheme, or a lavish, beribboned bouquet fit for a theatrical first night. A bunch of flowers can say many things, usually much more easily than any words could do, and with a great deal more style.

A successful bouquet should always look generous and full. Plenty of flowers and foliage should be used, and scented flowers included whenever possible. A bow or trailing ribbons add a special touch and usefully cover any wire or rubber band used to secure the stems.

Over the last decade or so, the style of bouquets has changed, with the emphasis now on a pretty mixture of flowers that look good together, and that can be put in a container to make an instant arrangement. This kind of bouquet is usually put together in the hand, each new bloom building the bunch up into the required shape.

Small posies in the Victorian style are still very popular and easy to make, whether from garden snippets or from simple flowers bought in a flower shop. They are best finished off with an edging of decorative leaves or frothy flowers, or with a collar of lace, paper or net.

A small gift can be
turned into a very special
present if it is
supplemented with
flowers. Here, the soft
hues of the wrapping
paper are echoed by the
colours of the flowers.

*MAIN TEXT PAGE 22*

Tiny posies of scented
flowers such as these
make irresistible gifts.
The range of possible
colour schemes and
flower combinations is
almost endless and most
gardens will yield
plenty of suitable
plant material.

*MAIN TEXT PAGE 22*

The palest pinks and blues combine in this trailing bouquet, which shows off the exquisite old-fashioned roses to perfection.

*MAIN TEXT PAGE 22*

Flowers in various shades
of pink are used in these
pretty bouquets for a
bride and her attendants.
A basketful of confetti
made up of fresh petals
stands to one side.

*MAIN TEXT PAGE 23*

The large white trumpet
lilies in this striking sheaf
of flowers for a modern
bride are deliciously
scented and simple in
shape and texture.

*MAIN TEXT PAGE 23*

Flowers make the perfect gift for any occasion. Whether you give a huge bunch of exotic flowers or simply a little posy contrived from a few garden blooms, the effect will always be pleasing.

There has recently been a move away from the formal, flat sheaf of florists' blooms over-wrapped in cellophane, impersonal and often quite hopeless to arrange. Many flower shops now put together a really pretty, relaxed bunch of mixed flowers, which can be wrapped with paper like a posy or simply finished off with a bow at the base. A bouquet of this kind can be placed straight in a vase for an instant flower arrangement.

If you are giving a wrapped present, it is nice to add a bunch of flowers which relates to the gift-wrapping. Here, a box covered in pretty floral paper is matched by the soft, delicate colours of a bouquet containing pinks, scabious, lisianthus and eryngium. When making up a bunch like this, mix the different types of blooms evenly and leave the stems as long as possible but neatly trimmed off at the ends. Secure them with a rubber band and cover this with a pretty ribbon.

Despite their fresh and youthful appearance, posies have a surprisingly long history. In medieval times, for example, nosegays of wild flowers and herbs, believed to have special properties, were often carried to ward off infection and disease, and to make life more fragrant in the less than sweet-smelling towns and villages of the day.

Posies can be made from any combination of flowers and foliage, although it is usually most rewarding to plan the colour scheme rather than simply to use a casual mixture. They are best made in the hand, starting with the central bloom and working round it. Further material may be added either at random or organised by shape and colour as you go.

Here on a rustic bench is a selection of posies all made from garden flowers picked in early summer. Roses feature strongly for their beautiful scent and lovely heads, while modest annuals such as cornflowers come into their own alongside golden roses and red alstroemeria. All-white or -cream posies look sophisticated and fresh, but a little green should always be added for contrast. A bunch combining different shades of pink and red is vibrant and unusual, as is a somewhat more daring mix of deep purples intermingled with crimson and lime green.

There can hardly be anything more special in the way of floral gifts than a bouquet of old-fashioned scented roses culled from a summer garden. The pretty, many-petalled blooms with their soft colours and wonderful fragrance have a romantic feel quite unlike that of any other flower and, if cut and treated properly (pages 116–117), will give many hours of pleasure after picking.

Pick any accompanying material carefully, selecting flowers with delicate colours and soft shapes and using varieties with smaller blooms to contrast with the large, round heads of the roses. Sprays of pinkish-mauve lilac, as here, work perfectly alongside the grey-blue speedwell flowers of veronica. A few delicately veined, hardy white geraniums have also been used, together with one or two pinks as fillers.

To make a bouquet like this, start with the longest flower stem as a base. Holding it loosely and head downwards, add further blooms one at a time, working up the bunch and fanning the flowers out wider nearer the top. The aim is to make a roughly triangular outline with the best blooms facing outwards. It is sometimes easier to work with the bunch resting on a surface, although you do still need to grip right round all the stems and to catch in each flower as you add it. Finally, secure the stems with a rubber band or piece of wire and finish off with a narrow ribbon.

A romantic bouquet of white roses is a perfect complement to a fairytale wedding dress such as this, with its falls of shimmering silk and decorations of tiny pearl heads and fabric bows. The roses used here are a garden variety called 'Iceberg', whose densely petalled, pure-white heads are held in clusters on long, stiff stems. Delicate trails of clematis leaves offset the blooms, falling naturally to the ground.

For a bouquet of this type it is probably best to wire the flowerheads, making them more manageable and easier to position. The wire is pushed a little way inside the end of each stem and wrapped with special tape. This hides the join and the whole length of wire, and keeps the flower fresh. The foliage stems should also be taped at the ends, so as to make a good, strong base for the arrangement. It is sensible to wire all the flowers before starting on the actual bouquet and to keep them fresh with the occasional gentle misting. When all the material has been assembled, the stems should be bound together with wire, wrapped with tape and bent into a handle shape. All this should be done as near as possible to the time of the wedding, but the flowers will keep perfectly well for a few hours.

There has been a revival in the lavish use of flowers in wedding bouquets, and many brides nowadays choose strong colours instead of the more traditional whites and creams. The flowers which the bride carries have to be the most spectacular, of course, followed by those for the older bridesmaids; the very young bridesmaids usually have something much smaller to suit their size.

Here, the smallest posy is based on the Victorian idea of concentric rings of different flowers. The centre is made from pure-white violets and these are surrounded by pink dianthus, themselves edged with a ruffle of delicate variegated leaves. Tightly taped to keep the flowers fresh, the stems are finished off with ribbon to make a comfortable handle.

The larger bouquet for a grown-up bridesmaid is a combination of country flowers and more formal elements, with a bunch of Queen Anne's lace and pale-pink London pride forming a base for many-petalled pink roses, dianthus and pink scented lilies. The flowers fall gracefully downwards and the stems are tied and taped at the top. Each bloom could have been wired for a stiffer, more ordered effect, and this has been done for the bride's bouquet, which includes sprays of white butterfly orchids, rich-pink lilies, pure-white stock and sweet peas in pink and white.

The strong, uncluttered shape of *Lilium longiflorum* makes it an ideal flower for a wedding bouquet, as does its heady fragrance. The white, waxy texture of the petals is offset by the golden-yellow stamens and by the hint of acid green at the base of the trumpet, echoed in this case by the green, globe-shaped flowers of *Viburnum opulus*, or the snowball tree. These look superb at the green stage, before they open out into much larger white spheres. The leaves are stripped from the woody stems, leaving only the flowers.

The bouquet here is simply a bunch or sheaf of flowers, each of which has been left unwired on its own stem. This relaxed arrangement is designed to be carried resting over one arm, with the stems supported by the opposite hand. The stems are bound securely below the flowers with wire, which is then covered with a band of fresh green leaves such as iris, pinned to hold it safe.

The smaller bunch of flowers, intended for a bridesmaid, uses the same viburnum blossoms, but this time with creamy-yellow calla lilies, deep-cream scented freesias and soft, grey-green whitebeam leaves. This is another simple bouquet, assembled in the hand stem by stem while turning the bunch in one direction and slightly twisting the stems to open out the flowers at the top. When all the blooms are in place, the stems are tightly secured and finished off with a ribbon.

# CHAPTER TWO

# FLOWERS FOR SPECIAL OCCASIONS

*A* special occasion can be as humble as a birthday celebration for two or as lavish as a grand reception. Whatever the scale of the event, flowers are essential. A wedding would be a strange affair indeed without them, and no party is complete without some kind of floral display around the house or on the buffet table. The arrangements do not have to be elaborate or extravagant to be successful, and it is often the simplest ideas that prove most effective.

A colour theme is important. It may come from the space that is being used or the food being served or, in the case of a wedding, the bride's dress. The time of year and availability of flowers will also influence the choice you make, but where possible at least a few garden flowers or material picked by you should be used to give the arrangements individuality and to avoid a standardised effect.

Included in this chapter are ideas for weddings, parties and celebrations throughout the year, from formal pedestal affairs for a party or reception, to festive winter decorations using dried flowers and a gold and silver colour scheme.

**I**f florists' foam, rather
than a vase or other
container, is used for an
arrangement, large areas
such as windowsills can
be copiously filled
with flowers for
maximum impact.

*MAIN TEXT PAGE 38*

The vibrant mix of reds
and pinks in this
arrangement is perfect
for late summer or early
autumn, when flowers
reach a peak of
colour intensity.

*MAIN TEXT PAGE 38*

An empty hearth is the
ideal setting for a richly
scented combination of
flowers which includes
both cut and uncut lilies,
the latter planted in
terracotta pots.

*MAIN TEXT PAGE 38*

A cotton floral fabric in various pastel colours sets the scene for this soft and pretty mix of blue, mauve and pink flowers.

*MAIN TEXT PAGE 39*

Flowers arranged along a
mantelpiece provide a
dramatic impact: this
formal area is decorated
with a relaxed
arrangement of
rich deep-pink and
red flowers.

*MAIN TEXT PAGE 39*

An original way to greet
guests is to hang a striking
arrangement of flowers in
a porch or doorway. This
spectacular decoration is
deceptively quick and
easy to make.

*MAIN TEXT PAGE 39*

Early summer flowers in
strong blues and yellows
are combined with fresh
green foliage in this
stunning basket
decoration that has been
stood on a pedestal.

*MAIN TEXT PAGE 52*

Classic white flowers are used on a large scale to fill the backdrop of this church altar in readiness for a spring country wedding.

MAIN TEXT PAGE 52

Candles combine
magically with warm
coral-coloured flowers in
this rich and romantic
decoration for a special
celebration.

*MAIN TEXT PAGE 52*

**L**oops and garlands of glossy green ivy comprise the main part of this Christmas decoration, with contrast being provided by pure-white trumpet lilies.

*MAIN TEXT PAGE 53*

The lily has an inherent grace and elegance that make it an easy flower to arrange. This classic vase contains a rich mixture of deep-pink 'Stargazer' lilies and shocking-pink nerines.

*MAIN TEXT PAGE 53*

50

For a formal occasion and for a house with a suitable setting such as a large entrance hall, a traditional pedestal decoration looks spectacular and timeless. Placing flowers on free-standing columns or pedestals is also a good idea when there is not enough room on top of the furniture for a large arrangement.

Make sure that the container used for the flowers is well balanced and secure on its base, with the extra insurance of wire or tape to hold it steady if necessary. Allow the flowers to fall gracefully downwards, and either make an all-round display for a large, open area or one for frontal viewing only if the pedestal is to stand at the side of a room.

In late spring, the choice of flowers is superb, including as it does the last of the bulbs such as tulips and the first of the summer flowers such as delphiniums. Here, the two are used alongside the fresh new leaves of beech and hosta, with yellow roses, alstroemeria, calla lilies, doronicums and sprays of white Queen Anne's lace also making an appearance. Twining through the whole arrangement are long stems of white *Clematis montana*, which have been allowed to spill downwards to soften the outline of this rather formal grouping. A simple, painted basket, large enough to hold the mass of damp foam needed for so many flower stems, has been used as the container.

A church wedding service is both solemn and celebratory, and the flowers used to decorate the church add very much to the overall effect and atmosphere.

It is often best to approach the decoration of a church by summing up the main features of the building and deciding which of these should be enhanced with flowers. For example, decorating pillars and windows and the altar itself is usually far more effective than dotting the church with pedestal arrangements, which never seem to integrate with the architecture.

A welcoming garland or swag in the porch or doorway is a lovely touch, while a spacious aisle can take posies or small bunches of flowers on the pew ends. Inevitably, however, the focal point is the altar, and this is where the most effort should be directed for a really memorable display. Many old churches are dark or have a lot of dark wood in their furnishings, so choose colours with care. Cream and white usually stand out best, and in any case many brides wish to keep to a traditional, all-white theme. Here, white flowers have been combined with a touch of cream and yellow and mixed with plenty of green foliage to offset the shape of the blooms. A range of flowers has been used to give a soft informality exactly suited to this small country church.

A special birthday or anniversary calls for something spectacular and extravagant in the way of floral decorations. Here, a very simple combination of flowers and foliage has been transformed into a truly sumptuous arrangement for a table.

Spending time on the colour scheme always pays off, and in this case the foliage is as important as the blooms. Soft, bluish-green rue leaves mix with lime-green sprays of molucella and provide a striking contrast to a mass of peach roses and coral spray carnations. Pale-cream roses with a blush of apricot make a perfect match for creamy alstroemeria streaked with peach and acid green.

To make this arrangement, use an oval tray as the starting point. Tape two blocks of damp foam to its base and insert the foliage, keeping each piece low and angled away from the centre of the tray. Next, add the roses, placing some low down and parallel to the table, but positioning the majority so as to face towards the front. Follow these with the alstroemeria and carnations, making sure to distribute the stems evenly throughout the arrangement. Lastly, make a few tiny posies out of rosebuds and carnations, bunching and wiring them firmly. Cut the stems short and wrap them in florists' tape. Pin the posies to a corner or edge of the tablecloth, or simply lay them down beside the main arrangement.

A traditional Christmas colour scheme of green, red and white always looks right, and if you can make use of seasonal evergreen foliage the effect is rich and opulent.

A carefully constructed swag or garland, with each small piece wired into place, is slow to make and fiddly to handle. Instead, find long stems of a climber such as glossy-leaved ivy, if you can, and wind thin, flexible rose wire along each length to make it more pliable. Join short pieces together with wire, if necessary, and for a more flamboyant effect twine shiny cord or ribbon along the swag among the leaves. Loop the garland under a shelf or mantelpiece, or hang it above a doorway or across a piece of furniture. Use masking tape or small pins to fix it where needed, and finish off with shiny artificial apples or tree decorations for a spark or two of colour.

Flower arrangements for traditional festivities are best kept simple so that they do not interfere with other decorations. Here, white longiflorum lilies, combined with a few stems of a purer white variety, are set off by a background of dark-green ivy and holly sprays, all assembled in a single block of damp foam standing in a protective tray.

Silver and gold look rich and festive and, mixed with the subtle colours of dried hydrangea flower-heads, make a luxurious-looking arrangement for winter.

Gathered in late autumn and left for drying, hydrangeas turn a whole range of beautiful and unusual colours, depending on their variety. Here, reddish-bronze heads have been sprayed lightly with silver lacquer paint, enough to frost the florets but not to obscure the natural colour. The shallow antique basket has been filled with a mass of these hydrangeas, mixed with a few dried poppy seed-heads and a spiky artichoke head, also dried. A gold cord bow adds the finishing touch. To continue the theme, a silver jug holds more of the silver flower-heads and, tucked in among them, silver glitter stars on wire stems.

Shallow bowls of floating night-lights look stunning among flowers, putting a lovely glow and sparkle on them. All the same, care should always be taken not to put lit candles too near dried flowers.

An arrangement like this does not always need fixing, but a block of dry foam does make the putting together easier and enables the whole thing to be moved from room to room. Do not be tempted to add too much silver or sparkle, but be subtle for a really glamorous effect. Try using different shades of gold ranging from yellow to red for an even warmer and richer look.

The lily has an inherent elegance and formality that make it a perfect choice for a classic table arrangement. The blooms last for a week or more and they grow old gracefully. To get maximum benefit out of them, always buy stems that have one or two flowers open and plenty more buds to follow.

The classic vase in this picture contains a rich mixture of deep-pink 'Stargazer' lilies and shocking-pink nerines. Plenty of space has been left around each head to give visual breathing space to the perfect blooms.

As an alternative, try using white lilies such as the trumpet-shaped *Lilium longiflorum*. They look good alone, but a few well-shaped pieces of green foliage, a spray of vine leaves and a few grey-green poppy heads will throw them into relief. Several stems of white nicotiana will echo the lily shapes and add their own special scent to the heady perfume of the lilies.

Pure-white trumpet lilies have a romantic, almost medieval look that is perfectly set off by old weathered oak, grey stone, polished wood and pewter. They also work well in a modern setting mixed with glossy surfaces such as chrome, glass, marble and plain white ceramic.

# CHAPTER THREE

# FLOWERS FROM THE PAST

Our view of how flowers were used and arranged in past times has to rely very much upon paintings of the period. What we do know is that people have always kept flowers in their houses, ranging, as today, from elaborate arrangements to a small pot on a windowsill containing a flowering bulb or plant dug from the garden.

Throughout every period and culture, flowers have inspired art and design in fabrics, ceramics, fashion, interior decoration and, of course, painting. It is fascinating to know that a plant such as the rose was loved and admired by the Romans, and that it continues to be enjoyed in this century. Flowers are a link through every age, and while we cannot always be sure of exactly how they looked in a particular period, it is interesting to guess at how they might have been employed, and to use this as an inspiration for an arrangement.

From a basketful of meadow flowers hinting at a medieval illustration to a thirties vase packed with period favourites, here, in the next few pages, are ideas to inspire the most avid floral historian. You do not have to live in a Georgian house to create an arrangement in the style of a Dutch painting, or a modern apartment to try out a swinging colour scheme: today, as in the sixties and seventies, anything goes.

The simplicity of flowers
from the past is captured
in this gentle combination
of cottage-garden and
roadside plants arranged
in a rustic wooden trug.

*MAIN TEXT PAGE 68*

The exquisite flower paintings of the 17th and 18th centuries provide an excellent source of inspiration to flower arrangers of today.

*MAIN TEXT PAGE 68*

The Victorians adored
roses, which looked
superb in their rich and
lavish interiors. Here, a
basket brimming with
heavy blooms sits on a
bedroom dressing table.

*MAIN TEXT PAGE 68*

Mauve, a favourite
thirties colour, has been
generously employed in
this evocative vaseful of
garden flowers, which has
been set against a
backdrop of wisteria.

*MAIN TEXT PAGE 69*

A surprising blend of
yellow, red and pink
flowers arranged in a
plain glass vase brings
vibrant colour to a
window seat.

MAIN TEXT PAGE 69

# CHAPTER FOUR

# TABLES AND MEALTIMES

Flowers and food combine happily, and the simplest meal can be turned into a feast with the addition of a mood-setting centrepiece or table arrangement.

Decorations for a buffet table can be as large and elaborate as you like, but where a sit-down meal is concerned, the flower arrangements should embellish without obscuring, leaving room for guests to talk to and see each other clearly. The flowers can follow through a colour scheme set by the china and linen, or they can provide a complete colour contrast or focal point. It is pleasant, too, to have scented flowers on a dining table, though the fragrance should not be so overpowering that it interferes with the smell and taste of the food and drink. Virtually any container able to hold water or foam, from a rustic basket to an elegant vase, may be used as a home for a table arrangement. On the other hand, the flowers may simply be inserted in blocks of foam disguised with moss or foliage. Here, in the following pages, are all kinds of stunning ideas, from a romantic, rose-filled table for two to a Victorian-inspired dinner setting of lavish drapes and tiers.

Hot pinks toned down with mauves and blues are the principal colours in this sturdy rustic basketful. The densely packed blooms create a rich pattern and texture.

*MAIN TEXT PAGE 84*

The acid green of
*Alchemilla mollis* provides a
sharp contrast to the
peach and cream of the
roses in this elegant
tea-time arrangement.

*MAIN TEXT PAGE 84*

Roses, honeysuckle and
mint add a delicious
fragrance to these elegant
twin arrangements, which
are ideal for a romantic
dinner for two.

*MAIN TEXT PAGE 84*

This exotic and vibrant
mix of mainly red flowers
is set out on a
correspondingly vivid
floral fabric with a black
background.

*MAIN TEXT PAGE 85*

Deep-red and butter-yellow roses have been combined with the trailing foliage of smilax in this sumptuous arrangement based on the Victorian idea of tiered epergne glasses.

*MAIN TEXT PAGE 85*

The colours of this lavish table arrangement for early summer take their cue from the surrounding orchard trees.

*MAIN TEXT PAGE 85*

In this rich, tapestry-like
decoration, a plentiful
harvest of late summer
flowers and fruit is
combined with the
stunning decorative
thistle-heads of garden
artichokes.

*MAIN TEXT PAGE 98*

Delicate sprays of Queen
Anne's lace prevent a big
arrangement such as this
from looking too solid
and heavy.

*MAIN TEXT PAGE 98*

The gleam of gold
enriches a wonderful
lustreware jug filled with
mixed roses. Pink
champagne adds a
frivolous note to this very
special party decoration.

*MAIN TEXT PAGE 98*

An old, warm toffee-brown, tin hat box makes a superb container for this autumn arrangement, which includes berries, rosehips and the trailing stems of ornamental vine.

*MAIN TEXT PAGE 99*

In winter when flowers
are scarce, glossy
evergreens and colourful
fruit can be used to add a
further dimension to
table decorations. A
stemmed *compotier* such as
the one used here makes
the perfect container.

*MAIN TEXT PAGE 99*

Just before the fresher colours of midsummer shift to the reds and golds of autumn, there is a point when deep purples, pinks and mauves reign supreme. Here is a glorious mixture of these late-summer hues, combined into a richly textured composition reminiscent of some glowing tapestry.

The main arrangement is set into a thirties ceramic vase, whose shape makes it very easy to position the flowers exactly as required, without recourse to florists' foam. To achieve such a result, begin with the largest pieces: tall spikes of larkspur and Michaelmas daisies, followed by stems of eryngium and purple liatris. Next, use all the medium-sized material: phlox, scabious and loose-bunched heads of blue brodiaea. Finally, add spray carnations, cornflowers and allium heads, making sure that the colours and shapes are well balanced.

Stand another, smaller, vase of flowers at the foot of the first, or use a plateful of handsome fruit and vegetables to create the impression of a still life. By picking out a colour from the main arrangement or adding another for contrast you can heighten the impact of the blooms enormously. Here, for example, a basket of globe-artichoke flowers, which will slowly dry out into excellent winter decorations, makes a vivid splash of electric mauve, greatly intensifying the general effect.

A soft mix of pink and white blooms makes a formal yet glamorous arrangement for a beautiful oak dining table. Generally, a centrepiece such as this should be low enough for dinner guests to be able to talk across it, but if the table is very large or long, or a formal seating plan restricts conversation to immediate neighbours, taller flowers may of course be used.

To create a similar effect, start by filling a shallow container, in this case an old copper preserving pan, with damp foam, enough to protrude slightly above the rim. Greenish-white Queen Anne's lace makes the perfect filler, and you should put this in place first, keeping the lower stems parallel to or just flush with the table. Next, use several stiff spikes of a miniature gladiolus to give emphasis and definition to the overall design, and to link the white of the Queen Anne's lace to the rich pink of the spray carnations. Add the carnations last of all and see that they are evenly distributed throughout the bowl, aiming for a smooth outline and a good viewpoint for every guest.

For a very special meal you could enhance the effect by laying a single pink bloom across each napkin or to one side of the cutlery, or else you might provide each place setting with its own delicate spray of flowers set in a tiny vase.

Gilded offerings make a truly sumptuous feast, and this buffet setting is no exception.

It is pleasing to have an overall colour scheme for any celebration, one encompassing food, flowers, china and cutlery, as well as candles and any other decorations. Here, a golden theme has been chosen for a birthday party, and careful thought has gone into co-ordinating all the decorative elements. Candlelight gives a warm, golden glow to the surroundings, while brass candlesticks add highlights and sparkle. The elaborate lustreware jug, piled round with a cluster of glittering Christmas-tree baubles and embellished with gold, makes a perfect container for a lavish show of mixed roses.

The flowers, in warm, soft shades of peach, pink, cream and yellow, have been arranged by colour, the small groupings making for a calmer effect than might be achieved with a random mix. Smaller bunches of roses, secured with a rubber band and trimmed to the same length, have been placed around the jug in its matching wash-bowl, filled with a shallow layer of water. No other flowers have been used, resulting in a rich and opulent display.

Here, the richness of autumn colours has been translated into an arrangement for a relaxed supper party, in which the earthiness of crusty bread combines with the russet tones of country cider, and bowlfuls of fruit make a generous appearance.

Scrubbed pine provides a perfect background for the brown china, baskets and wooden boards used to display the food. The flowers chosen for the arrangement, and placed in a large, salt-glazed mixing bowl, are equally simple and straightforward, combining alstroemeria in a deep, rusty red and gold with vivid orange lilies and yellow roses – a mixture echoing the colours of the fruit. A note of fresh green is afforded by a few leafy vine stems, added at the last possible minute, which are anchored in the bowl and trailed gently round to encircle the table and make a garland for the meal.

If the arrangement needs to last several hours, it is perhaps more convenient to use foliage such as smilax, which keeps well in or out of water. The vine leaves, though, do look particularly suitable in this context, whether wreathing the buffet, decorating the crockery or serving as verdant little plates for items such as cheese.

Sometimes the tone and shape of a container can suggest a style and colour theme for a flower arrangement. Here, the smooth, painted surface of an old metal hat box seemed perfect for an extravagant mixture of warm orange and apricot hues, combining bought and garden-grown flowers with rich clusters of early autumn berries. Spicy shades of orange, brown and terracotta need a touch of green to stay fresh and natural-looking, and in this case long trails of an ornamental vine with just a hint of autumn colouring have been used to contrast with the fussier flowers. A container like this, not designed to hold water, should first be lined to make it waterproof, then filled with damp foam to support the flower stems.

Pale-orange rowan berries are among the first to ripen and they last well on the stem, cut and used in arrangements. Here they have been used with the small, clustered fruits of a type of hypericum and some large ornamental rosehips. The flowers are a blend of spray chrysanthemums, carthamnus, spray carnations, and the yellow button flowers of wild tansy. A few sprays of *Alchemilla mollis* add a sharp note of citrus green, and plenty of natural foliage has been left on the stems of the roses, rowan and hypericum. To emphasize the warm golden tones of the flowers and berries, a plate of late apricots has been placed beside the flowers.

When flowers are scarce and expensive during the winter months, add colour with fruit and use glossy evergreen leaves such as ivy to create a rich, traditional look. Make use of candlelight to enhance the warm colours and beautiful textures of grapes, peaches and melons, and for a special Christmas meal drape a tablecloth and decorate it with bunches of flowers and leaves.

Here, a Victorian *compotier* filled with fruit ready for eating has been transformed into a delightful centre-piece with the aid of flowerheads and clusters of leaves fitted in among the fruit. To make a similar arrangement, start with a layer of regular-sized pieces such as small apples. Secure them with a little florists' putty if required. Pile up more decorative fruits into a pyramid, starting with the largest items, for example melons or mangoes. Try to arrange a bunch of grapes so that it hangs over the edge of the dish. When you have finished with the fruit, add the flowers and leaves. These can simply be tucked into place, the stems slotting under pieces of fruit where appropriate.

To achieve the draped effect, use two cloths, one on top of another. Catch the topmost one up at the table edge between place settings and secure it with pins. Finally, fix small posies to the bunched fabric, both to conceal the pins and to provide a lovely finishing touch.

# OUTDOOR ARRANGEMENTS

*I*t might seem a little strange to talk about outdoor flower arrangements, but there are all kinds of occasions when you might need more blooms outside than a garden can normally provide. Imagine, for example, a summer wedding reception held on a lush green lawn, or a midsummer buffet party or evening barbecue with tables set up and lanterns in the trees, and you will soon see why. To add to this, many gardens are nowadays furnished to become an extension of the living area of a house, so it makes sense to plant and arrange garden pots in the way you might plan flower decorations for an indoor situation.

Flowers used outside will have to work hard to compete with all the plants already growing there, and since daylight tends to drain colours, they will need to be darker and stronger in hue than usual. Arrangements on tables should be anchored down with plenty of weight at the base of the container, top-heavy shapes liable to topple over at the first breath of wind obviously being out of the question. If the weather is very warm, they will need frequent topping up with water, as they will obviously dry out quickly in sunlight or breezy conditions. Most important of all, use should be made of strong, sturdy containers suitable for their surroundings: the garden is no place for delicate porcelain or flimsy stemmed glass.

A boldly printed fabric provided the inspiration for this vibrant party arrangement, which is reminiscent of the tropics.

*MAIN TEXT PAGE 114*

The wedding flowers set
out on this tulle-covered
table are delicate and
romantic to fit the mood
of the occasion.

*MAIN TEXT PAGE 114*

The colours of early
spring flowers are bright
and light. Here, a sunny
combination of yellow,
white and green flowers
has been placed in a
correspondingly fresh
and leafy setting.

MAIN TEXT PAGE 114

106

An elaborate and very
decorative punchbowl
makes the perfect
container for a mass of
brightly coloured, early
summer roses.

MAIN TEXT PAGE 115

The soft whites and
creams of the flowers in
this romantic setting
blend naturally into the
green landscape.

*MAIN TEXT PAGE 115*

The inspiration for this garden fantasy was a richly patterned fabric swirling with leaves, flowers and birds. A group of vases filled with vivid blooms such as these would make a perfect decoration for an evening buffet or garden party, producing an almost tropical effect. The flowers are actually very simply arranged, relying on the fusion of bright, clashing colours and combination of strongly shaped, single-toned vases for their impact.

Choosing suitable containers and deciding which flowers to put where is usually the hardest part, but one that is worth getting right. Here, the strong orange in the tablecloth has been picked as the basic colour for the display, and orange lilies make a bold start in the larger turquoise jug, mixed with several of the pink 'Stargazer' variety and a few tall stems of larkspur. The coral-pink, spherical vase contains a handful or two of orange nasturtiums and shocking-pink pelargonium flowers, while its neighbour holds a mix of golden-yellow alstroemeria, dark-centred garden marigolds and more of the orange lilies. The smaller turquoise container has most of the lily blooms, this time combined with purplish allium heads, rich-pink roses and paler-pink daisies.

It is a very special occasion indeed that warrants all the effort of a full-scale buffet meal laid outdoors, but if the weather permits there is nothing quite so glamorous or memorable as a wedding feast held on green lawns or in the shelter of a marquee. To live up to the day the flowers, too, must be worth remembering, yet they should not detract from the lovely setting or the beautiful food; in this case just two varieties have been used.

Foamy gypsophila, or baby's breath, casts wonderful shadows and patterns, and is light and airy enough not to be in the way or to obscure the food. It is a most attractive flower, but it is generally used merely as a filler, with its delicate beauty overpowered and concealed. A cloud of gypsophila on its own, on the other hand, is a spectacular sight, one perfectly suited to a wedding celebration.

To add to the soft, dreamy atmosphere, lengths of white bridal net have been looped along the sides of the table and caught up at its edge with single scabious heads. More of these pale-mauve blooms, cut short and dotted about the table in tumblers, have been used to provide a subtle note of colour.

Plain glass containers are best where a suitably insubstantial effect is required, as here. If the flowers are kept in them for any length of time, the water should be changed as soon as it loses its sparkle.

Nature in springtime is replete with brilliant greens, sharp, acid lemons, soft yellows and brilliant golds. White is prominent, too, in orchard blossoms and garden flowers, and has a purity and brightness that echo the feel of the season.

Look out at this time of year for bunches of fat ranunculi in shades of yellow and white. With their tight, round buds and many-petalled heads, their green eyes and golden stamens, these relations of the humble buttercup make superb cut flowers, lasting well and adding a rich period quality to any arrangement. Tulips and irises emphasize the feeling of spring, while sweet jonquils give scent and texture with their clustered heads. A delicate contrast to the solid roundness of these flowers, and a welcome relief from all the yellows, is provided by the cool petals of white honesty.

Here, a lime-green sponged bowl makes the perfect container for an armful of these spring flowers, enlivened with a little fresh green foliage. Blocks of damp foam have been used inside the bowl, since a densely packed structure of this kind needs plenty of support.

There is a magical moment in mid-summer when the colours of flowers and fruit seem to reach a crescendo, and when everything looks divine. Cherries are ripe and strawberries are plentiful, and nearly every garden you see has its share of full-blown roses. The grass is still a lovely green, and for a week or two things will stay brilliant and fresh. Now is a perfect chance to enjoy the fruits of the season.

Here, an extravagant and extraordinary punchbowl, decorated with a kaleidoscope of ceramic flowers, has been put to a use for which it was never intended and filled to overflowing with a mass of summer roses. Blooms from the flower shop jostle alongside their country cousins in colours ranging from palest apricot and pinkish-mauve to butter-yellow and purest white, while a note of salmon-pink is provided by a few stems of scented sweet peas. In this arrangement there seems to be no need for any greenery other than the small amount naturally present among the flower-heads, but one or two trails of bryony from the hedge-row have been added to fall gently to the table below.

A plateful of seasonal fruit can be as good to look at as any bunch of flowers. Choose under-ripe, un-blemished pieces and pile them on to a pretty plate. Stand them beside the flower arrangement to enjoy their visual qualities, then eat them as you like.

A summer country wedding calls for soft and romantic flowers. In these arrangements, set out on a rustic buffet table, the colour scheme of white, cream and green blends naturally into the landscape.

The arrangements have been set in tall-stemmed glass containers to hold the flowers off the table and give a floating effect. Trails of foliage have turned the conventional grouping into something spectacular, with bryony, clematis and vine leaves trailing across the table and down on to the grass.

The basis of the arrangements is off-white spray roses and pure-white perennial lavatera. A few single white roses with golden centres add emphasis, while small clusters of white daisies on long spikes and long, lime-green tassels of *Amaranthus caudatus* 'Viridis' provide lightness without weight.

The small size of all these flowers keeps the arrangements elegant and pretty, and at the same time dainty enough for a table setting where food and drink will be present. Low, flat table decorations can be set out among food, but flowers on a pedestal are best kept to the back or side of a buffet table to prevent them from being knocked over.

Growing plants in tubs and containers provides an opportunity to move things about and to create outdoor flower arrangements both temporary and permanent. Plants such as fuchsias do very well in pots, and their flowering period can extend over a whole summer season.

A small, paved seating area, here backed by a low stone wall, is sheltered and secluded and makes a perfect spot in which to arrange a particularly colourful and pretty selection of flowering pots. In a garden which concentrates on foliage for its effect throughout the year, it is important to have an area or two of more specialised colour. Pink has been chosen here, and it comes in all shades, from the palest version in the case of the daisies to the brilliant two-colour hues of the pelargonium 'Paton's Unique', planted in large old terracotta pots.

Most fuchsia varieties have cascading flowers and some have branches which droop gracefully downwards. These types are particularly useful for hanging pots or baskets, which show their habit off to advantage. Grown as standard bushes on a tall, single stem, fuchsias can also make lovely trees, tall enough to stand among other pots and create height and fullness. They do not relish very dry conditions or strong sunlight and actually prefer a certain amount of dappled shade.

# FLOWER CARE

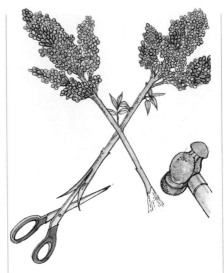

## *CUTTING AND CONDITIONING FLOWERS*

### CUTTING FLOWERS

Garden flowers are best cut in the early morning or evening, when transpiration is at its lowest. On a hot, sunny afternoon, they will naturally have less moisture in their cells and therefore be more prone to wilt. As flowers always benefit from a long drink before they are used, this may determine just when they are gathered. Ideally, a drink overnight is perfect if they are to be used the next morning, so evening picking is probably best. Always gather flowers quickly and put them into water as soon as possible. Choose fresh, healthy blooms just coming into full flower, or in slightly open bud. Condition the flowers as described below.

### BUYING FLOWERS

Shop-bought flowers are usually conditioned before they are sold, but you can still re-cut the stems under water yourself. Make sure you buy flowers from a shop or stall that has a quick turnover and fresh supplies brought in from markets at least twice a week.

### CONDITIONING

**1** Cut flower stems at a sharp angle, so that the maximum area of the cut end is exposed to the water. Do this under water if possible.

**2** Peel back a little of the bark of woody stems of shrubs and trees, then hammer or split the first inch or so to allow the water to penetrate easily. This can be done with a hammer, sharp garden secateurs or strong scissors.

**3** Stand the prepared flowers in a bucket filled with warm water and leave them to have a long drink for several hours or overnight.

**4** If the stems are bent and you want to straighten them, wrap the flowers tightly in newspaper and plunge into water. This method is particularly effective for flowers such as tulips and gerbera.

**5** Certain flowers exude a milky sap which interferes with their water intake. The stems of flowers such as poppies, euphorbia and ferns can be sealed by singeing the ends over a flame.

**6** Some flowers, for example poppies, will last longer if their stems are plunged into a small amount of boiling water for a few minutes.

**7** The large, hollow stems of flowers such as delphiniums and hippeastrums can be filled with water and then plugged with a small piece of cotton wool. Stand the stems in water straight after this treatment.

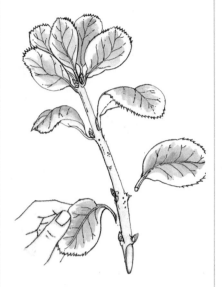

**8** Always strip the lower leaves off stems so that they do not sit under water in the vase. Rotting leaves will pollute the water and encourage the creation of bacteria, cloudy water and an unpleasant smell.

**9** Roses should have all their thorns removed, as well as any extra leaves and small branches. Strip the thorns off the stems with the blade of a pair of scissors, or use a tool available specially for this purpose.

**10** Some lilies have pollen-laden stamens that can brush against clothes and furnishings and stain indelibly. To prevent this, carefully snip out the stamens.

**11** If flowers wilt unexpectedly, try reviving them by recutting the stems and standing them in shallow hot water for about half an hour. Position the flowers away from the steam when adding the water.

**12** A good method of conditioning foliage is to immerse it completely in water for a few hours. Do not use this method on grey- or silver-leaved foliage, or on any plants that have woolly foliage.

**13** Remove the topmost buds of flowers such as gladioli to ensure that the lower buds will open.

## TOOLS AND EQUIPMENT

**CUTTING TOOLS**
Among the most essential tools for flower arranging are a pair of good-quality secateurs or special florists' scissors with short blades.

### WIRE

A selection of different kinds of wire is useful. Stiff stub wire is excellent for dried flower arrangements, and a reel of fine rose wire is handy for many jobs. Chicken wire can be used as a support for large and heavy stems in a vase.

### WATERING EQUIPMENT

A long-spouted watering can is useful for reaching into large arrangements. Many flowers enjoy a fine, hazy mist of water, so include a spray mister among your equipment.

### TAPE

If you are making posies and bouquets you may need the special tape available for binding stems and wrapping around wires. Often known as gutta-percha tape, it comes in green, white and brown.

### FLORISTS' FOAM

Blocks of wet foam for supporting fresh flowers in shallow containers are indispensible, as are blocks of the special type of foam available for dried flower arrangements. Both types of foam can be cut to any shape and size, and can easily be concealed, if necessary, with a layer of moss.

Most of the wet foam available today can be soaked in a minute or so. Allow the foam to stand above the edge of your container if you wish to add extra height to the flowers. Tape or wire the foam in position if necessary, or push it down on to a special florists' spike anchored with adhesive clay to the bottom of the container. Foam does not look good in glass containers unless it is covered or hidden in some way, so save these for simple and informal arrangements.

If cut at an angle, most stems will push easily into damp foam and will stay firmly put. However, if you are using plants with very soft stems you may need to spike holes first in the foam, into which the stems can then be inserted.

Flowers take up a lot of water, so remember to keep the foam damp by topping up the container with fresh water occasionally, particularly in warm conditions.

## SUPPORTS FOR PLANTS

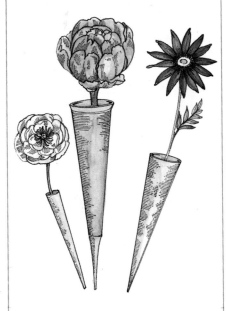

### FUNNELS

If you are planning a really grand, large-scale arrangement for a special occasion, long funnels will be useful for adding extra height to individual flower stems.

**PINHOLDERS**

Pinholders — heavy, metal blocks with sharp spikes — are an old-fashioned but good way of securing some arrangements. Attach them to the bottom of the container with florists' putty or plasticine, then insert the flowers among the spikes.

**CHICKEN WIRE**

Crumpled chicken wire is useful for supporting plants in narrow-necked vases and shallow bowls, particularly if you are using large, woody-stemmed branches and top-

heavy flowers. It can be jammed in place, or else wired or taped inside the container to keep it secure.

**MARBLES**

Clear glass marbles make a pretty addition to a glass vase and help hold stems in position. Pebbles can be used for the same purpose.

**TWIGS**

To secure stems in exactly the right position in a container, cut a twig into small pieces and use these as a wedge or prop.

---

### PROLONGING THE LIFE OF AN ARRANGEMENT

If your flowers have been conditioned well and arranged in damp foam or water, they should last for a week or more depending on the variety. To help them last longer, always remember to keep the parts of the stems that are under water free from leaves, and use slightly warm water, never icy cold. Add a drop or two of bleach and a teaspoon of sugar to the water, or use the special crystals often provided by florists with cut flowers which help to prolong flower life. Replace the water after a few days if it is getting stale and remove and discard any plant material that is obviously tired, fading or dead. Cut out spent blooms and leave the buds to open out.

*The charts that follow list the characteristics of over 100 plants commonly used in flower arranging. The natural flowering period for each plant is given, although it should be noted that many of the plants are also available from florists at other times of the year.*

# FLOWER DATA

| PLANT | AVERAGE LENGTH OF CUT STEMS | SHAPE AND TEXTURE | COLOURS | SCENT | DAYS AS CUT FLOWER | PLANT TYPE | FLOWERING PERIOD |
|---|---|---|---|---|---|---|---|
| *Acanthus mollis* Bear's breeches | 2–3 ft (60–90 cm) | Tall, nodding, spiky flowers. Large, glossy leaves | Mauve-white | None | 7–14 | Perennial | Summer |
| *Achillea* Yarrow | 2–4 ft (60–120 cm) | Stiff clusters of flowers, up-turned on stems | Yellow | None | 7 | Perennial | Late summer/ autumn |
| *Agapanthus* African lily | 1–2 ft (30–60 cm) | Globes of many small, trumpet-shaped flowers on long, thick stems | Blue, white | None | 7–10 | Perennial | Summer |
| *Alchemilla mollis* Lady's mantle | 1 ft (30 cm) | Tiny frothy flowers. Pretty leaves | Acid greenish-yellow | None | 7–14 | Perennial | Early to late summer |
| *Allium* Decorative onion | 1–3 ft (30–90 cm) | Globe-shaped heads of small, starry flowers on stiff stems | White, cream, mauve, purple, yellow, pink, cerise | Onion scent | 7–10 | Bulb | Early summer to autumn |
| *Alstroemeria* Peruvian lily | 1–2 ft (30–60 cm) | Clusters of small, lily-type flowers on long stems | Pink, red, yellow, orange, peach, purple | None | 7–14 | Perennial | Summer |
| *Althaea rosea* Hollyhock | 1–3 ft (30–60 cm) | Tall, straight stems with flat rosettes of flowers | Pink, white, maroon, red, salmon, cream | None | 7 | Biennial | Summer |
| *Amaranthus caudatus* Love-lies-bleeding | 6–12 inches (15–30 cm) | Furry tassels in clusters on plant | Maroon, green | None | 7 | Annual | Summer |
| *Anaphalis* Pearl everlasting | 1–2 ft (30–60 cm) | Clusters of flowers on lax stems | White | None | 7 | Perennial | Late summer/ autumn |
| *Anchusa* Alkanet | 1¼–3 ft (35–90 cm) | Tiny flowers. Bristly leaves | Blue | None | 7 | Perennial | Spring/early summer |
| *Anemone* Windflower | 6–12 inches (15–30 cm) | Cup-shaped flowers on stiff stems | Purple, red, white, blue | None | 7–14 | Perennial | Best in spring and autumn |
| *Antirrhinum majus* Snapdragon | 1–3 ft (30–90 cm) | Spikes of nodding flowers along stems | Yellow, white, red, pink, orange | None | 7–10 | Annual | Summer |
| *Aquilegia* Columbine/ granny's bonnet | 1–3 ft (30–90 cm) | Nodding flowers. Well-shaped leaves | Blue, white, mauve, purple, pink | None | 7–10 | Perennial | Spring/early summer |
| *Aster ericoides* September flower | 1–2 ft (30–60 cm) | Tiny, starry daisies | White, yellow | None | 7–10 | Perennial | Summer |
| *Aster novi-belgii* Michaelmas daisy | 1–3 ft (30–90 cm) | Clusters of daisy-like flowers | Mauve, cerise, white, pink, purple | None | 7–10 | Perennial | Autumn |
| *Astrantia* Masterwort | 1–2 ft (30–60 cm) | Small, star-like flowers | Pinkish-white | None | 7–10 | Perennial | Spring/early summer |

| PLANT | AVERAGE LENGTH OF CUT STEMS | SHAPE AND TEXTURE | COLOURS | SCENT | DAYS AS CUT FLOWER | PLANT TYPE | FLOWERING PERIOD |
|---|---|---|---|---|---|---|---|
| Azalea | 6–12 inches (15–30 cm) | Clusters of exotic flowers on woody stems | Yellow, pink, orange, red, white, peach | Some varieties very scented | 5–7 | Evergreen shrub | Spring/early summer |
| Borago officinalis Borage | 1 ft (30 cm) | Tiny, star-shaped flowers. Rough leaves | Deep blue | None | 5–7 | Annual | Late spring/ summer |
| Brodiaea | 6–9 inches (15–25 cm) | Clusters of small, tubular flowers | Blue | None | 7–10 | Bulb | Spring/ summer |
| Calendula officinalis Pot marigold | 6–12 inches (15–30 cm) | Daisy-like, many-petalled flowers | Shades of orange | Spicy | 7–10 | Annual | Summer |
| Camellia | 6–12 inches (15–30 cm) | Dramatic, single or double, rose-shaped blooms | Pink, white, red, peach | None | 7 | Evergreen shrub | Early spring to early summer |
| Campanula Bell flower | 6–24 inches (15–60 cm) | Bell flowers along stems | Blue, white mauve, pink | None | 7–10 | Biennial or perennial | Summer |
| Catananche caerulea Cupid's dart | 1–2 ft (30–60 cm) | Daisy-like flowers on thin, stiff stems | Sky-blue | None | 7–14 | Perennial | Summer |
| Centaurea cyanus Cornflower | 6–12 inches (15–30 cm) | Daisy-like, many-petalled flowers | Deep blue, also white, pink, mauve | None | 7–10 | Annual | Summer |
| Cheiranthus Wallflower | 6–12 inches (15–30 cm) | Spikes of flowers on stiff stems | Rust, red, orange, yellow, bronze, purple | Very scented | 7 | Biennial | Spring |
| Chrysanthemum frutescens | 6–12 inches (15–30 cm) | Daisy-like flowers. Delicate foliage | White, yellow | None | 7–10 | Annual or perennial | Summer |
| Chrysanthemum parthenium Feverfew | 6–12 inches (15–30 cm) | Clusters of daisy-like flowers with yellow eyes. Pretty foliage | White flowers. Pale green or lime-green foliage | Distinctive | 7–10 | Perennial | Spring/ summer |
| Clarkia Godetia | 1–2 ft (30–60 cm) | Two or three soft-petalled trumpets on each stem | Pink, red, white, salmon, scarlet | None | 7 | Annual | Summer |
| Convolvulus tricolor | 6–8 inches (15–20 cm) | Delicate, trumpet-shaped flowers on short stems | Deep blue with yellow-white centres | None | 7 | Annual | Summer |
| Convallaria majalis Lily-of-the-valley | 6–8 inches (15–20 cm) | Tiny bells on short stems | White | Very scented | 7 | Perennial | Spring |
| Cosmos Mexican aster | 1–2 ft (30–60 cm) | Daisy-like flowers with large eyes | Yellow, rust, brownish-red, pink, white | None | 7–10 | Annual | Late summer |
| Crocosmia x crocosmiiflora Montbretia | 6–12 inches (15–30 cm) | Small, trumpet-shaped flowers on sides of wiry stems | Orange, red, yellow | None | 7 | Bulb | Late summer |

| PLANT | AVERAGE LENGTH OF CUT STEMS | SHAPE AND TEXTURE | COLOURS | SCENT | DAYS AS CUT FLOWER | PLANT TYPE | FLOWERING PERIOD |
|---|---|---|---|---|---|---|---|
| Dahlia | 6–24 inches (15–60 cm) | Ball- or daisy-shaped, many-petalled flowers on stiff stems | Red, orange, yellow, pink, white, peach | None | 7–10 | Perennial | Late summer |
| Delphinium ajacis Rocket larkspur | 1–3 ft (30–90 cm) | Spikes of many florets. Stiff stems | Blue, pink, white, mauve, cerise | None | 7–14 | Annual | Summer |
| Delphinium elatum | 2–5 ft (60–150 cm) | Tall spikes covered with flowers | White, blue, mauve | None | 7–14 | Perennial | Summer |
| Dianthus barbatus Sweet william | 6–24 inches (15–60 cm) | Clusters of small flowers | Red, white, bi-colours, pink | Unusual scent | 7–10 | Biennial | Summer |
| Dianthus caryophyllus Carnation/ gilliflower/ clove-pink | 1–2 ft (30–60 cm) | Frilly balls on stiff stems | White, red, shades of pink, peach | Slight scent | 10–14 | Perennial | Summer |
| Dianthus (garden varieties) | 8–12 inches (20–30 cm) | Small, frilled or plain flowers | Red, white, bi-colours, pink, laced | Warm, spicy scent | 7–10 | Perennial | Summer |
| Digitalis Foxglove | 2–3 ft (60–90 cm) | Hooded, hanging bells on long stems | Purple, mauve, white, pink, apricot, cream, yellow | None | 7 | Biennial or perennial | Early summer |
| Echinops Globe thistle | 2–3 ft (60–90 cm) | Balls of thistle flowers | Silvery-mauve | None | 7–14 | Perennial | Late summer |
| Eremurus Foxtail lily | 2–3 ft (60–90 cm) | Spikes of densely packed, spiky flowers | Yellow, white, orange | None | 7–10 | Perennial | Summer |
| Eryngium Sea holly | 2–3 ft (60–90 cm) | Spiky thistle-heads. Fine, handsome leaves | Silvery-blue, mauve | None | 7–10 | Perennial | Late summer |
| Euphorbia Spurge | 1–3 ft (30–90 cm) | Clusters of bracts on stems | Lime-green, green, orange | None | 7 | Perennial | Winter to summer |
| Euphorbia marginata Snow on the mountain | 1–2 ft (30–60 cm) | Variegated foliage and bracts | Cream-green | None | 7–10 | Annual | Summer |
| Foeniculum vulgare Fennel | 1–2 ft (30–60 cm) | Umbellifer flowers. Ferny foliage | Yellow | Strong scent | 7 | Perennial | Summer |
| Forsythia Golden-bell | 1–3 ft (30–90 cm) | Small, starry flowers along bare branches | Yellow | None | 7 | Shrub | Early spring |
| Freesia | 6–12 inches (15–30 cm) | Up to eight trumpet-shaped flowers on each stem | Yellow, white, mauve, pink | Very scented | 7–10 | Bulb | Winter/spring |
| Fritillaria imperialis Crown imperial | 1–2 ft (30–60 cm) | Crown of drooping, trumpet-shaped flowers | Yellow, orange | Strange, strong scent | 7 | Bulb | Spring |

| PLANT | AVERAGE LENGTH OF CUT STEMS | SHAPE AND TEXTURE | COLOURS | SCENT | DAYS AS CUT FLOWER | PLANT TYPE | FLOWERING PERIOD |
|---|---|---|---|---|---|---|---|
| *Galanthus nivalis* Common snowdrop | 6 inches (15 cm) | Drooping, tubular flowers. Grass-like leaves | White | Very faint | 7 | Bulb | Winter/early spring |
| *Galium odoratum* Sweet woodruff | 6 inches (15 cm) | Very small, starry flowers | White | Strong as it dries | 7 | Perennial | Spring |
| *Gardenia jasminoides* Cape jasmine | 6–12 inches (15–30 cm) | Many-petalled, flattish blooms. Glossy ever-green foliage | White | Very scented | 7 | Greenhouse evergreen shrub. Hardy in warm climates | Summer |
| *Genista* Broom | 1–2 ft (30–60 cm) | Bushy stems covered in small, pea-shaped flowers | Cream, yellow, pink, peach, red, mauve | Quite scented | 7 | Shrub | Summer |
| *Gerbera jamesonii* Transvaal daisy | 1–2 ft (30–60 cm) | Daisy-like flowers on stiff stems | White, cream, pink, yellow, orange, peach, red | None | 7–14 | Greenhouse perennial. Hardy in warm climates | Summer |
| *Gladiolus* Sword lily | 1–3 ft (30–90 cm) | Spires of trumpet-shaped, soft-petalled flowers | White, cream, yellow, red, orange, peach, pink, mauve | None | 7–14 | Perennial | Summer |
| *Gypsophila* Baby's breath | 1–2 ft (30–60 cm) | Bushy stems covered in tiny, frothy balls of flowers | White | None | 7–14 | Annual or perennial | Summer |
| *Helianthus annuus* Sunflower | 2–5 ft (60–150 cm) | Large, dramatic, daisy-like flowers | Orange, yellow, rust | None | 7–10 | Annual | Summer to autumn |
| *Helichrysum bracteatum* Everlasting/ straw flower | 1–2 ft (30–60 cm) | Crisp, straw-textured, daisy-like flowers | Red, yellow, orange, pink, terracotta, white, cream, burgundy | None | 10–14 | Annual | Summer |
| *Helleborus* Christmas rose/ Lenten rose/ hellebore | 1–3 ft (30–90 cm) | Clusters of bracts. Fine leaves | Green, purple white | None | 7–10 | Perennial | Winter/early spring |
| *Hemerocallis* Day lily | 2–3 ft (60–90 cm) | Large, trumpet-shaped flowers opening singly | Orange, yellow, peach | None | 7 | Perennial | Summer |
| *Heuchera sanguinea* Coral bells/ coral flower | 6–12 inches (15–30 cm) | Tiny, nodding flowers on thin stems | Red, white, pink, coral | None | 7 | Perennial | Late spring/ summer |
| *Hippeastrum* Amaryllis | 1–3 ft (30–90 cm) | Three to five enormous, lily-like flowers on large, hollow stem | White, peach, pink, red | Some white types scented | 7–14 | Greenhouse bulb | Winter/spring |
| *Hyacinthus* Hyacinth | 6–12 inches (15–30 cm) | Waxy, solid flowers packed on flower spike | Blue, pink, white, cream, cerise, red | Strong scent | 7–10 | Bulb | Spring |

| PLANT | AVERAGE LENGTH OF CUT STEMS | SHAPE AND TEXTURE | COLOURS | SCENT | DAYS AS CUT FLOWER | PLANT TYPE | FLOWERING PERIOD |
|---|---|---|---|---|---|---|---|
| Hydrangea | 1–2 ft (30–60 cm) | Large mop-head of bracts on shortish stems | Pink, white, blue, red | None | 7 | Shrub | Late summer |
| Iris (large species) Flag | 6–24 inches (15–60 cm) | Exotic blooms on long, stiff stems | Maroon, blue, mauve, yellow-white, green | None | 7 | Perennial | Early summer |
| Jasminum nudiflorum Winter-flowering jasmine | 6–24 inches (15–60 cm) | Single, starry flowers along arching stems | Yellow | None | 5–7 | Shrub | Winter |
| Jasminum officinale Common white jasmine | 6–12 inches (15–30 cm) | Starry flowers on trailing stems | White | Very scented | 5–7 | Climber | Summer |
| Lathyrus odoratus Sweet pea | 6–12 inches (15–30 cm) | Delicate, butterfly-like flowers | White, pink, mauve, cream, red, scarlet, maroon, purple | Very strong scent | 7–10 | Annual | Summer |
| Lavandula Lavender | 6–12 inches (15–30 cm) | Tiny flowers on top of stiff stems | Purple, mauve | Very strong scent | 7–10 | Evergreen shrub | Summer |
| Lavatera trimestris Mallow | 8–18 inches (20–45 cm) | Trumpet-shaped flowers in clusters | Pink, white | None | 7–10 | Annual | Summer |
| Liatris pycnostachya Blazing star | 1–2 ft (30–60 cm) | Tufts of shaggy petals on straight spikes | Rosy-purple | None | 7–10 | Perennial | Summer |
| Lilium Lily | 1–2 ft (30–60 cm) | Exotic, large blooms with big stamens | Pink, orange, yellow, white, peach, cerise | Many varieties have a very strong scent | 7–10 | Bulb | Summer |
| Lonicera Honeysuckle | 6–12 inches (15–30 cm) | Long, narrow trumpets at tops of stems | Yellow, cream, pink, red | Strong scent | 5–7 | Climber or shrub | Summer/ autumn |
| Lupinus polyphyllus Lupin | 1–2 ft (30–60 cm) | Stiff spires covered in nodding, pea-shaped flowers | Blue, mauve, purple, yellow, peach, red, pink, cream, bi-colours | Strong but not very pleasant | 7 | Perennial | Early summer |
| Mahonia japonica Mahonia | 6–12 inches (15–30 cm) | Dangling strings of blossoms. Spiky foliage | Yellow | Strong | 5 | Evergreen shrub | Winter/early spring |
| Matthiola incana Stock | 1–2 ft (30–60 cm) | Spikes of blossoms cover stiff stems | Cream, pink, white | Strong scent | 7–10 | Biennial or short-lived perennial | Summer |
| Moluccella laevis Bells of Ireland/shell flower | 1–2 ft (30–60 cm) | Stiff spires of spiny bracts | Lime-green | None | 7 | Annual | Late summer |
| Monarda didyma Sweet bergamot/ Oswego tea/ bee balm | 1–2 ft (30–60 cm) | Hooded flowers in coronet around top of each stem | Red, deep pink | Slight (more intense when crushed) | 7 | Perennial | Summer |

| PLANT | AVERAGE LENGTH OF CUT STEMS | SHAPE AND TEXTURE | COLOURS | SCENT | DAYS AS CUT FLOWER | PLANT TYPE | FLOWERING PERIOD |
|---|---|---|---|---|---|---|---|
| *Muscari armeniacum* Grape hyacinth | 6 inches (15 cm) | Clusters of tiny bells in cone shape on stems | Blue, white | None or very slight | 7 | Bulb | Early spring |
| *Myosotis* Forget-me-not | 6 inches (15 cm) | Tiny flowers along stem among soft leaves | Blue | None | 7 | Biennial | Spring to early summer |
| *Myrrhis odorata* Sweet cicely | 6–12 inches (15–30 cm) | Umbellifer flowers. Ferny, soft leaves | Creamy-white | When crushed | 7 | Perennial | Early summer |
| *Narcissus* Daffodil/ jonquil | 6–12 inches (15–30 cm) | Trumpet-shaped flowers with collar of petals. Grass-like leaves | Yellow, white, cream | Some species scented | 7–10 | Bulb | Spring |
| *Nemophila menziesii* Baby blue eyes | 6 inches (15 cm) | Tiny flowers on weak stems | Blue | None | 5–7 | Annual | Summer |
| *Nepeta* Catmint | 6–24 inches (15–60 cm) | Small, hooded flowers along arching stems | Mauve | Slight | 7 | Perennial | Summer |
| *Nerine bowdenii* | 12–18 inches (30–45 cm) | Trumpet-shaped flowers at top of stiff stems | Shocking pink, red | None | 7–10 | Bulb | Autumn |
| *Nicotiana* Tobacco plant | 1–2 ft (30–60 cm) | Soft-petalled, trumpet-shaped flowers | Cream, white, green, pink, purple, maroon | Very strong in some varieties | 7 | Annual | Summer |
| *Nigella damascena* Love-in-a-mist | 6–8 inches (15–20 cm) | Delicate petals with ruff of soft spikes | Blue | None | 7 | Annual | Summer |
| *Ornithogalum nutans* Star of Bethlehem | 6 inches (15 cm) | Starry flowers in clusters | White, grey, green | None | 5–7 | Bulb | Early spring |
| *Paeonia* Peony | 8–18 inches (20–45 cm) | Many-petalled or single flowers with large centres of stamens | Pink, red, cream, white, deep maroon | None | 7 | Perennial | Early summer |
| *Papaver nudicaule* Iceland poppy | 1 ft (30 cm) | Large, papery-petalled flowers | Yellow, white, orange, red, cream, peach | None | 7 | Biennial | Summer |
| *Papaver orientale* Oriental poppy | 1 ft (30 cm) | Papery petals around black stamens | Red, peach, white, pink | None | 5 | Perennial | Early summer |
| *Papaver paeoniaeflorum* Peony-flowered poppy | 1–1½ ft (30–45 cm) | Very full, peony-like, papery petals. Large, ornamental seed-heads | Pink, red, white, mauve | None | 5 | Annual | Summer |
| *Papaver rhoeas* Field poppy/ shirley poppy | 8–12 inches (20–30 cm) | Delicate, papery, single or double petals | Pink, red, white, peach, bi-colours | None | 5 | Annual | Summer |

| PLANT | AVERAGE LENGTH OF CUT STEMS | SHAPE AND TEXTURE | COLOURS | SCENT | DAYS AS CUT FLOWER | PLANT TYPE | FLOWERING PERIOD |
|---|---|---|---|---|---|---|---|
| *Pelargonium* Geranium | 6–12 inches (15–30 cm) | Simple flowers in clusters from branched stems | Red, pink, white, purple, salmon | None (except scented leaf varieties) | 5–7 | Greenhouse sub-shrub. Hardy in warm climates | Spring/ summer/ autumn |
| *Phacelia* Blue bonnet | 8 inches (20 cm) | Bell-shaped, upturned flowers | Blue | None | 5–7 | Annual | Summer |
| *Philadelphus* Mock orange | 6–24 inches (15–60 cm) | Small, white flowers close to stems | White | Very scented | 7 | Shrub | Summer |
| *Phlox* | 6–24 inches (15–60 cm) | Clusters of flowers on top of stiff stems | White, pink, red, mauve | Scented | 7 | Perennial | Summer |
| *Polygonatum* Solomon's seal | 1–2 ft (30–60 cm) | Arching stems with small, tubular flowers | White-green | None | 7 | Perennial | Early summer |
| *Primula* (large varieties) Primrose/ polyanthus/ auricula/ cowslip | 6–8 inches (15–20 cm) | Clusters of flat flowers on top of stems | Red, yellow, orange, white, pink, green, lemon | Many very scented | 7 | Perennial | Spring |
| *Pulmonaria* Lungwort | 6–12 inches (15–30 cm) | Small flowers among hairy leaves | White, blue-pink, red | None | 7 | Perennial | Winter/early spring |
| *Ranunculus* Buttercup | 6–12 inches (15–30 cm) | Many-petalled, buttercup-shaped flowers | Red, orange, pink, yellow, white, cream, salmon, maroon | None | 10–14 | Perennial | Summer |
| *Rhododendron* | 6 inches–3 ft (15–90 cm) | Exotic, trumpet-shaped flowers. Woody stems | Mauve, pink, red, salmon, white | Some varieties scented | 5–10 | Evergreen shrub | Late winter to early summer |
| *Rosa* (many varieties) Rose | 6–24 inches (15–60 cm) | Single, semi-double or double-petalled flowers, usually on thorny stems | Red, white, pink, yellow, cream, apricot | Strong in many varieties | 7 | Shrub, climber or rambler | Summer/ autumn |
| *Rosmarinus officinalis* Rosemary | 6–12 inches (15–30 cm) | Tiny, hooded flowers along stems with spiky leaves | Mauve, blue | Strong when crushed | 5–10 | Evergreen shrub | Spring/ summer |
| *Rudbeckia* Coneflower/ black-eyed Susan | 1–2 ft (30–60 cm) | Daisy-like flowers on long stems | Yellow, orange | None | 7 | Annual or perennial | Late summer |
| *Ruta graveolens* Rue | 6–12 inches (15–30 cm) | Ferny foliage. Insignificant flowers | Leaves grey-green | When crushed | 7 | Evergreen sub-shrub | Summer |
| *Salvia* Sage | 6–24 inches (15–60 cm) | Hooded flowers along stems. Hairy leaves | Red, purple, blue | Foliage scented in some varieties | 7 | Annual or perennial | Summer |
| *Saxifraga* x *urbicum* London pride | 6–12 inches (15–30 cm) | Tiny, frothy flowers on straight stems | Pale pink | None | 7 | Perennial | Spring |

| PLANT | AVERAGE LENGTH OF CUT STEMS | SHAPE AND TEXTURE | COLOURS | SCENT | DAYS AS CUT FLOWER | PLANT TYPE | FLOWERING PERIOD |
|---|---|---|---|---|---|---|---|
| *Scabiosa* Pincushion flower/scabious | 1–2 ft (30–60 cm) | Flat, many-petalled flowers | Mauve, blue, pale yellow, white | None | 7 | Perennial | Summer |
| *Scilla* Squill | 6 inches (15 cm) | Clusters of starry flowers | Blue | Faint | 7 | Bulb | Spring |
| *Sedum* (large varieties) Stonecrop | 6–24 inches (15–60 cm) | Clusters of small flowers forming a flat-topped cone | Pink, mauve, red | None | 7 | Perennial | Late summer/ autumn |
| *Solidago* Golden rod | 1–2 ft (30–60 cm) | Clusters of small flowers forming bushy sprays | Yellow, gold, lemon | None | 7–10 | Perennial | Late summer |
| *Spiraea* | 6–24 inches (15–60 cm) | Small, fluffy flowers on shrubby twigs | Pink, red, white | None | 7 | Shrub | Summer |
| *Stachys lanata* Lamb's ears | 8 inches (20 cm) | Woolly, decorative leaves. Flowers on long spikes | Grey-green leaves. Pink or purple flowers | None | 7 | Perennial | Summer |
| *Stephanotis floribunda* Madagascar jasmine | 6–12 inches (15–30 cm) | Waxy, tubular flowers on twining stems | Cream | Very strong scent | 7–10 | Greenhouse evergreen climber. Hardy in warm climates | Spring to autumn |
| *Syringa* Lilac | 1–2 ft (30–60 cm) | Conical clusters of many small flowers on woody stems | Mauve, purple, white | Very strong scent | 7 | Shrub | Early summer |
| *Tropaeolum majus* Nasturtium | 6–8 inches (15–20 cm) | Trumpet-shaped flowers on succulent stems | Yellow, flame, orange, red, cream, bi-colours | Slightly spicy | 7 | Annual | Summer |
| *Tulipa* Tulip | 6–12 inches (15–30 cm) | Long, chalice-shaped flowers | Yellow, white, green, pink, red, orange, apricot | None | 7–10 | Bulb | Spring |
| *Veronica* Speedwell | 6–12 inches (15–30 cm) | Tiny flowers along stems | Mauve, blue, white | None | 7 | Perennial | Early summer |
| *Vinca* Periwinkle | 6–12 inches (15–30 cm) | Flat, round or star-shaped flowers on lax stems. Good foliage | Blue, mauve, white | None | 7 | Evergreen trailing shrub | Early spring to summer |
| *Viola odorata* Sweet violet | 6 inches (15 cm) | Five-petalled flowers on short stems. Heart-shaped leaves | Purple, mauve, white | Faint and sweet | 7 | Perennial | Spring |
| *Viola tricolor* Heartsease *Viola* x *wittrockiana* Garden pansy | 6–8 inches (15–20 cm) | Five-petalled flowers with large, velvety petals | Purple, white, mauve, blue, orange, yellow | None | 7 | Perennial | Winter/spring/ summer |
| *Zantedeschia aethiopica* Arum lily | 1–2 ft (30–60 cm) | Trumpet-shaped, waxy flowers on thick stems | White, yellow green | None | 7–10 | Perennial | Summer |

*See also* plant lists on pages 120–127.

# A

Achillea 38, 68
Agapanthus 38, 39, 84
Akebia leaves 39
*Alchemilla mollis* 38, 74, 84, 99
Allium 98, 114
Alstroemeria 22, 38, 39, 52, 85, 99, 114
*Amaranthus caudatus* 'Viridis' 115
*Amaryllis belladonna* 84
Aquilegia 39, 68, 69, 85
Artichoke (flower) 86, 98

# B

Basket arrangements 40, 52, 56, 60, 68, 72, 84, 85
Beech leaves 39, 52, 85
Bouquets 8–23
Brodiaea 38, 98
Bryony leaves 115
Bunches 8–23
Buttercup 68
Buying flowers 116

# C

Calla lily 23, 52
Campion 68
Carnation 52, 69, 74, 84, 98, 99
Carthamnus 99
*Carthamnus tinctoris* 38
Centaurea 38
Chicken wire 118, 119
Chive flowers 69
Christmas decorations 46, 53
Chrysanthemum 69, 99
Church flowers 42, 52
Clematis 84
Clematis 'Perle d'Azur' 39
Clematis leaves 23, 115
*Clematis montana* 52
Conditioning flowers 116–17
Cornflower 22, 39, 68, 98
Cutting flowers 116

# D

Dahlia 69
Daisy 114, 115
Delphinium 52, 68, 69, 116
Dianthus 23
Doorway arrangements 36, 39
Doronicum 52

# E

*Echinops ritro* 38, 39
Eryngium 22, 39, 84, 98
Eucalyptus leaves 39
Euphorbia 116

# F

Fabrics 32, 39, 78, 84, 102, 114
Ferns 116
Fireplace arrangements 30, 38
Florist's foam 118
Flower balls 39
Flower care 116–119
Foliage 96
Foliage conditioning 117
Forget-me-not 69
Foxglove 68, 85
Fragrant flowers 84
Freesia 23, 84
Fruit 68, 86, 92, 96, 98, 99, 115
Fuchsia 85, 115
Funnels 118

# G

Geranium (cranesbill) 22, 38, 68, 69
Gerbera 116
Gift-wrapping 10, 22
Gladiolus 38, 69, 98, 117
Gypsophila 114

# H

Hemerocallis 68
Hippeastrum 116
Holly 53
Honesty 114
Honeysuckle 68, 76, 84, 85
Hosta leaves 52
Hyacinth 69
Hydrangea 48, 53
Hypericum 99

# I

Iris 64, 69, 114
Ivy 46, 53, 99

# J

Jasmine 84
Jonquil 114

# L

Larkspur 38, 39, 98, 114
Lavatera 115
Liatris 98
Lilac 22, 69
*Lilium longiflorum* 23, 53
*Lilium regale* 38
Lily 20, 23, 30, 38, 39, 46, 53, 85, 99, 114
Lily, care of 117
Lily 'Pink Beauty' 38
Lily 'Stargazer' 50, 53, 114
Lisianthus 22
London pride 23, 85
Love-in-a-mist 68

# M

Mallow 38
Mantelpiece arrangements 34, 39
Marbles 119
Marigold 114
Michaelmas daisy 38, 84, 98
Mint leaves 76, 84
Mirrors 38
Molucella 52

# N

Nasturtium 114
Nerine 50, 53
Nicotiana 53
Nosegays 22

# O

Orchid 23
Outdoor arrangements 100–15

# P

Paintings as inspiration for arrangements 6, 58, 68
Pansy 69
Pebbles 119
Pedestal arrangements 40, 52, 115
Pelargonium 114
Pelargonium 'Paton's Unique' 115
Peony 68, 84
Philadelphus 84
Phlox 98
Pinholders 119
Pink 22, 38, 84
Poppy 38, 39, 53, 68, 84, 85, 116
Posies 9, 12 22, 23, 52
Pot-grown plants 30, 38, 112, 115

# Q

Queen Anne's lace 23, 39, 52, 68, 88, 98

# R

Ranunculus 64, 69, 85, 114
Reflective surfaces 38
Rhododendron 39
Rose 14, 16, 22, 23, 38, 39, 52, 60, 68, 69, 74, 76, 80, 84, 85, 90, 98, 99, 108, 114, 115
Rose, care of 117
Rose 'Constance Spry' 69
Rose 'Iceberg' 23
Rose 'Mme Grégoire Staechelin' 69
Rosehips 94, 99
Rowan berries 94, 99
Rue leaves 52

# S

Scabious 22, 38, 68, 98, 114
Secateurs 117
Smilax 80, 85, 99
Snowball tree 23
Solidago 38
Solomon's seal 68
Spry, Constance 69
Statice 38
Stock 23, 85
Supports for flowers 118–19
Sweet pea 23, 39, 69, 85, 115

# T

Table decorations 52, 53, 70–99
Tansy 99
Tape (gutta-percha) 118
Tools 117–18
Tulip 39, 52, 69, 85, 114, 116
Twigs, as supports 119

# V

Veronica 22
*Viburnum opulus* 23
Vine leaves 53, 94, 99, 115
Viola 69
Violet 23

# W

Wallflower 85
Watering equipment 118
Wedding flowers 16–21, 23, 42, 52, 104, 114, 115
Weigela 39
Whitebeam leaves 23
Window arrangements 26, 38, 66
Wire 118
Wisteria 62, 69

ACKNOWLEDGMENTS
The publishers wish to thank Barbara Baran and Peter Moloney for their help in the preparation of this volume.